OCTAVIA E. BUTLER

POWER OF THE PEN

BLACK WOMEN WRITERS

by Joyce Markovics

NORWOOD HOUSE PRESS

NORWOOD HOUSE PRESS

For more information about Norwood House Press, please visit our website at: www.norwoodhousepress.com or call 866-565-2900.

Book Designer: Ed Morgan
Editorial and Production: Bowerbird Books

Photo Credits: © MILBERT ORLANDO BROWN/KRT/Newscom, cover, title page, 5; © Les Howle, 6; Wikimedia Commons/Chicago History Museum, 7; Wikimedia Commons/Doctor Doctorstein, 8; © Les Howle, 9; Wikimedia Commons/Joost J. Bakker from IJmuiden, 10; © Les Howle, 11; Wikimedia Commons/Marian Wood Kolisch, Oregon State University, 12; Courtesy Clarion West, 13; Library of Congress, 14; freepik.com, 15, 16; Wikimedia Commons/Nikolas Coukouma, 17; freepik.com, 18; © Les Howle, 19; NASA/JPL-Caltech/University of Arizona, 21.

Hardcover ISBN: 978-1-68450-669-9
Paperback ISBN: 978-1-68404-976-9

Library of Congress Cataloging-in-Publication Data

Names: Markovics, Joyce L., author.
Title: Octavia E. Butler / by Joyce Markovics.
Description: [Buffalo] : Norwood House Press, 2024. | Series: Power of the pen: Black women writers | Includes bibliographical references and index. | Audience: Grades 4-6
Identifiers: LCCN 2023045981 (print) | LCCN 2023045982 (ebook) | ISBN 9781684506699 (hardcover) | ISBN 9781684049769 (paperback) | ISBN 9781684049820 (ebook)
Subjects: LCSH: Butler, Octavia E. | American fiction--African American authors--Biography--Juvenile literature. | Science fiction--Women authors--Biography--Juvenile literature. | African American novelists--Biography--Juvenile literature. | African American women authors--Biography--Juvenile literature. | LCGFT: Biographies. | Picture books.
Classification: LCC PS3552.U827 Z78 2024 (print) | LCC PS3552.U827 (ebook) | DDC 813/.54 [B]--dc23/eng/20231003
LC record available at https://lccn.loc.gov/2023045981
LC ebook record available at https://lccn.loc.gov/2023045982

372N--012024

Manufactured in the United States of America in North Mankato, Minnesota.

CONTENTS

INTRODUCING OCTAVIA

Octavia E. Butler created new worlds. She imagined fantastic stories and characters. Over time, Octavia became one of the world's best science fiction writers. And she reshaped the **genre** to include Black people. When Octavia began writing, "I wasn't in any of this stuff I read," she said. So, "I wrote myself in." Through writing, Octavia found her voice. She wrote from the point of view of her characters. She also revealed truths about human nature. Long after her death, her books are still praised. Octavia's impact is as powerful as she was.

ASK YOURSELF
YOUR IMAGINATION IS A POWERFUL TOOL. HOW DO YOU USE YOUR IMAGINATION?

Octavia Butler won many important awards during her life.

SCIENCE FICTION, OR "SCI-FI" FOR SHORT, IS A GENRE OF IMAGINATIVE STORY. IT'S OFTEN BASED ON SCIENCE AND **TECHNOLOGY** OF THE FUTURE.

EARLY YEARS

Octavia Estelle Butler was born on June 22, 1947, in Pasadena, California. She was an only child. Her father shined shoes to make a living. Her mother, also named Octavia, was a maid. When Octavia was very young, her father died. Her grandmother, Estella, stepped in to help raise her.

Throughout her life, Octavia struggled with dyslexia (diss-LEK-see-uh). This is a difficulty in reading where a person may see letters or words in the wrong order.

Estella was a determined woman. She raised seven children on a **plantation** in Louisiana. And she taught them to read and write. In the 1920s, Estella saved enough money to move her family to California. She and Octavia's mother were strict but loving. Octavia's mother read stories to her every night. When Octavia was six, her mother said, "Here's the book. Now you read." Soon, Octavia learned to read on her own.

This Black Southern family is arriving in Chicago during The Great Migration.

FROM 1910 TO 1970, MILLIONS OF BLACK PEOPLE LEFT THE SOUTH. THEY MOVED TO THE NORTH AND WEST. THEY WERE ESCAPING **RACIAL** VIOLENCE. THEY WERE ALSO LOOKING FOR BETTER JOBS AND OPPORTUNITIES. THIS WAS CALLED THE GREAT MIGRATION.

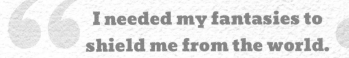

I needed my fantasies to shield me from the world.

When Octavia started school, she was very shy. As an only child, "I was comfortable with adults," she said. "I had no idea how to get along with other children." Octavia remembers the first time another kid called her "ugly." She was in first grade. "I was different. And even in the earliest grades, I got pounded for it," said Octavia. "I wanted to disappear."

Octavia spent a lot of her free time reading at the Pasadena Central Library, shown here.

ASK YOURSELF
CAN YOU THINK OF A TIME WHEN SOMEONE MADE FUN OF YOU? HOW DID IT FEEL?

So, Octavia kept to herself. In elementary school, a teacher said that Octavia "dreams a lot" in class. It was true. Octavia wrote down her dreams in a big pink notebook. Those dreams eventually became stories. "I was lonely," said Octavia. "But when I wrote, I wasn't." She loved writing about animals, especially horses. When Octavia saw a pony being abused at a local carnival, she wrote about it. Though, in her story, a wild horse **shapeshifts** to avoid being caught by humans.

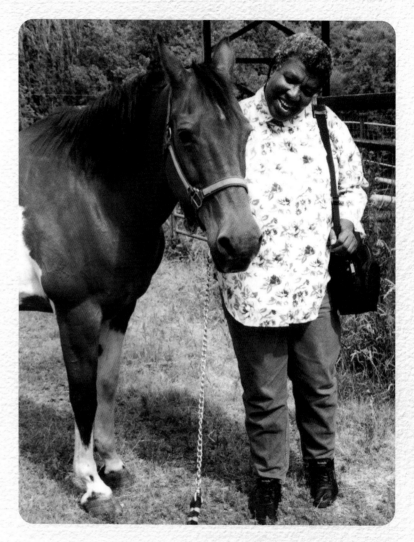

Even as an adult, Octavia loved horses. Here she is with a horse named Morning Star.

9

Octavia recalls the first science fiction movie she ever saw. It was *Devil Girl from Mars*. The movie is about Nyah, a female alien who can control minds. Octavia remembers thinking, *I can write a better story than that!* She then started **drafting** what would become her *Patternist* novels. At the time, Octavia knew exactly what she wanted to be. She didn't set out to become a science fiction writer. "I wanted to be a *writer*," Octavia said.

The character Nyah in *Devil Girl from Mars* uses a ray gun like this one.

In 1965, Octavia graduated from high school. Then she went to college and got an **associate's degree**. During that time, Octavia kept writing. She won a short-story contest. This fueled her passion. However, Octavia also needed money to live. So, she had "lots of horrible little jobs." But these jobs gave Octavia time to imagine new stories. She carried small notebooks and wrote in them every day.

When Octavia wasn't working, she enjoyed being in nature.

OCTAVIA WORKED MANY ODD JOBS. ONE JOB WAS A DISHWASHER. ANOTHER WAS A POTATO CHIP INSPECTOR! HOWEVER, SHE STILL MADE TIME TO WORK ON STORIES. MANY NIGHTS, OCTAVIA GOT UP AT 2 OR 3 A.M. TO WRITE.

HER WORK

Writing and working shaped Octavia's days. To improve her skills, she took writing classes. One of her teachers, Harlan Ellison, who was also a science fiction writer, liked Octavia's work. He invited her to attend a science fiction writers' group in Pennsylvania. It was known as the Clarion Workshop. There, Octavia made friends with other writers. And she sold a couple of her short stories!

ASK YOURSELF
WHY IS IT IMPORTANT TO PRACTICE SOMETHING?

The science fiction writer Ursula K. Le Guin was a big inspiration to Octavia.

12

With newfound confidence, Octavia worked on her *Patternist* novels. The three-book series is about beings with **telepathic** powers. The books explore issues of power, slavery, and freedom. In 1976, she **published** her first book, *Patternmaster*. **Critics** liked the book overall. "The author carefully spells out the ground of her unique world," one wrote.

Octavia (far right) with her classmates at her first Clarion Workshop

OCTAVIA WORKED ON THE *PATTERNIST* SERIES FOR FIVE YEARS. DURING THAT TIME, OCTAVIA **VOLUNTEERED** AS A TUTOR AT THE LIBRARY. WHEN ASKED WHY, SHE SAID, "I WANT TO HELP."

> **Strength. Endurance. To survive, my ancestors had to put up with more than I ever could. Much more.**
> –Dana, *Kindred*

In 1979, Octavia published *Kindred*. "I wanted to write a novel that would make others feel the history: the pain and fear that Black people have had to live through," she said. In the book, Dana, the main character, travels back in time. She goes to an 1800s plantation in Maryland. There, she's forced into slavery. Octavia went to Maryland to research her novel. Every detail had to be right. She wanted her readers to know what it was like to be enslaved. Octavia also wanted to **portray** enslaved people as the heroes they were.

This photo shows enslaved people on a plantation in 1862.

Kindred became a bestseller. Harlan Ellison described it as "that rare magical **artifact**." In 1984, Octavia won a Hugo Award for best science fiction short story. She also traveled around the world researching her new books. In the 1980s, Octavia published the *Xenogenesis* (zen-OH-jen-uh-sis) **trilogy**.

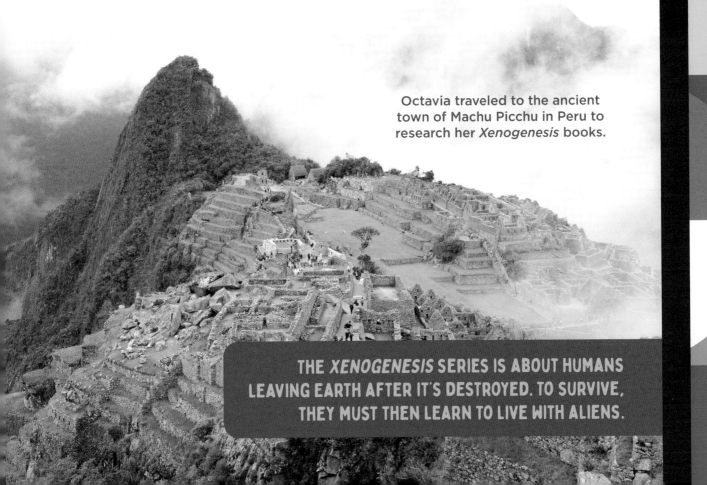

Octavia traveled to the ancient town of Machu Picchu in Peru to research her *Xenogenesis* books.

THE *XENOGENESIS* SERIES IS ABOUT HUMANS LEAVING EARTH AFTER IT'S DESTROYED. TO SURVIVE, THEY MUST THEN LEARN TO LIVE WITH ALIENS.

> **We human beings make a lot of the same mistakes over and over again.**

In the 1990s, Octavia published another book series. The first book was *Parable of the Sower*. It takes place in the 2020s. Climate change has driven Americans from their homes. And drug use and gun violence are widespread. The novel follows Lauren, a teenager, who can feel the pain of others. She dreams of a better world. So, she creates a new religion called Earthseed. One of the beliefs is "Embrace **diversity**. . . . Or be destroyed."

The Parable of the Sower of the Seed is a story from the Bible. In it, seeds represent the teachings of God. A sower is someone who plants seeds.

ASK YOURSELF
HAVE YOU EVER IMAGINED A DIFFERENT WORLD? WHAT WOULD IT BE LIKE?

The final book, *Parable of the Talents*, follows Lauren's story. It tells of a ruthless leader who forces his religion on America. He also brings back slavery. Octavia said these novels were about power and the abuse of it. "The only way to prove to yourself that you have power is to use it," said Octavia. If people try, she believes they have the power to save themselves—and the world.

Octavia signs a copy of one of her many books.

OCTAVIA KEPT WINNING AWARDS FOR HER WORK. SHE BECAME THE FIRST SCIENCE FICTION WRITER EVER TO WIN A MACARTHUR FELLOWSHIP, A HUGE PRIZE. OCTAVIA WAS FLOORED. "THIS ISN'T REAL," SHE SAID.

> **Every story I create, creates me. I write to create myself.**

In 1996, Octavia's mom got sick and died. Octavia was heavy with grief. "I wrote nothing of value for some time," she said. A few years after her mom died, Octavia got back to work. In 2000, she won the PEN Lifetime Achievement Award. More and more people started paying attention to her work.

Frustrated by her writer's block, Octavia still pushed herself to write every day.

Octavia wrote and published *Fledgling*, her last novel. It's about a community of vampires and humans. The main character, Shori, seeks **justice** for her family after they are killed. While writing *Fledgling*, Octavia felt ill. She was tired and had trouble breathing. "I'm not functioning," she wrote in 2004. "I sit and drowse a lot." On February 24, 2006, Octavia Butler died at her home. She was 58 years old.

Octavia (far right) became a teacher at the Clarion Workshop. Here she is in 2005— a year before her death.

IT'S THOUGHT OCTAVIA DIED FROM A STROKE. A STROKE OCCURS WHEN BLOOD CAN'T FLOW TO THE BRAIN. WITHOUT BLOOD FLOW, THE BRAIN WILL DIE.

OCTAVIA'S POWER

Octavia was truly a **visionary**. Today, she is remembered for her incredible stories. She wrote more than a dozen books, some of which are only gaining in popularity. A few have been made into graphic novels and TV shows. Others are being turned into movies. In her writing, Octavia talked about race, **gender**, and power. Despite the flawed world she often wrote about, she was always hopeful. "There is nothing new under the sun but there are new suns," Octavia wrote. Steven Barnes, a science fiction writer, said about Octavia, "She opened a door and walked all the way through it." By doing so, she "created a path for others."

OCTAVIA HELPED CREATE AFROFUTURISM. IT'S A GENRE THAT COMBINES SCIENCE FICTION, HISTORY, AND FANTASY TO EXPLORE THE BLACK EXPERIENCE.

Octavia E. Butler Landing

In 2021, NASA named a place on Mars the Octavia E. Butler Landing site.

TIMELINE AND ACTIVITY

June 22, 1947
Octavia is born in Pasadena, California

1968
Octavia receives an associate's degree

1976
Octavia publishes her first book, *Patternmaster*

1979
Octavia publishes *Kindred*

1984
Octavia receives one of two Hugo Awards

1993
Octavia publishes *Parable of the Sower*, the first of two books in a series

2005
Fledgling, Octavia's last book, is published

February 24, 2006
Octavia dies at age 58

GET WRITING!

Octavia E. Butler is famous for her science fiction. Imagine a far-off world that's different from Earth. What creatures live there? What are they like? Write a short story about that world. Share your work with an adult or friend!